Illustrated by JAMES E. BARRY

Let's Learn About

SUGAR

by MAUD and MISKA PETERSHAM

HARVEY HOUSE, INC.
Publishers
Irvington-on-Hudson, N. Y.

*The authors are indebted to Elizabeth Morton, formerly
Trade Book Editor of The John C. Winston Company,
for her able updating of this new edition of "Sugar"*

Library of Congress Catalog Card Number: 69-10755
Manufactured in the United States of America

HARVEY HOUSE, INC. • *Publishers*
Irvington-on-Hudson • New York

Contents

A Cave Boy Discovers Honey

Long, long ago, at the time men were living in caves, a boy stood near his home in the rocks. He noticed a bear cub sniffing about the trunk of a hollow tree.

As he watched, he saw the little cub begin to climb the tree. There was a big hole in the tree trunk, and when the cub reached the opening, he stopped and sniffed again. Then he stuck his paw into it and pulled out a piece of honeycomb that was dripping with sweet, golden honey.

He began to eat it greedily as he clambered down. He was fat and clumsy, so before he had time to reach the ground, a great swarm of angry, wild bees flew out of the hole.

The frightened bear dropped his honeycomb and dashed off, howling. The buzzing, stinging bees chased after him.

The boy who had been watching wanted to find out what it was that had tasted so good to the little bear. He crept up to the tree and carefully picked up the piece of comb that the cub had dropped.

Something sticky oozed from it and stuck to his fingers. He took a tiny taste. It was sweet and delicious. He ran back to the cave with the dripping comb. He had found out that honey was sweet and good to eat.

From earliest days, primitive men gathered honey from the comb of the wild honeybee. They prized it very highly as food, and for thousands of years it was the only sweet they knew.

9

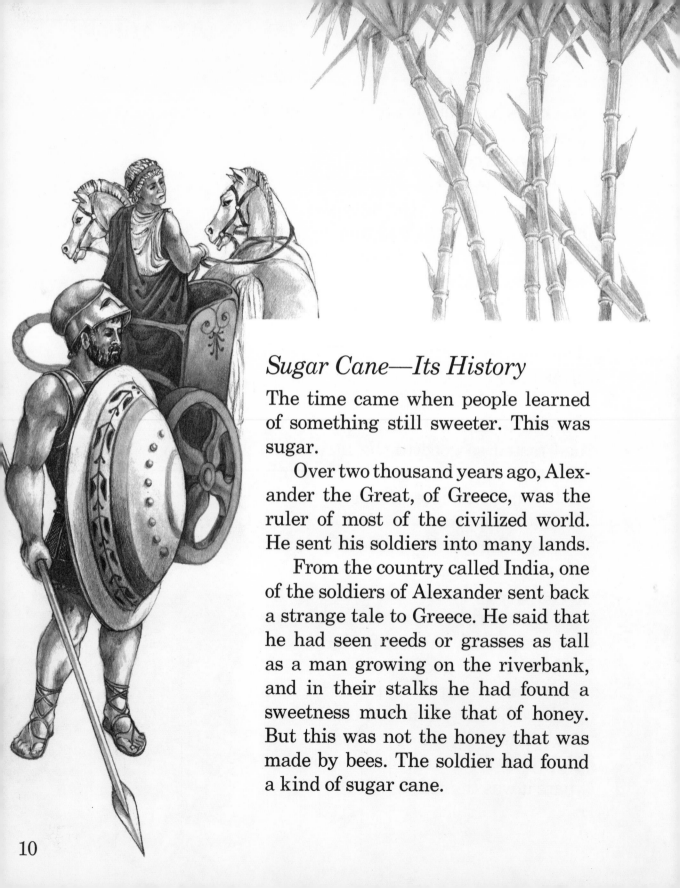

Sugar Cane—Its History

The time came when people learned of something still sweeter. This was sugar.

Over two thousand years ago, Alexander the Great, of Greece, was the ruler of most of the civilized world. He sent his soldiers into many lands.

From the country called India, one of the soldiers of Alexander sent back a strange tale to Greece. He said that he had seen reeds or grasses as tall as a man growing on the riverbank, and in their stalks he had found a sweetness much like that of honey. But this was not the honey that was made by bees. The soldier had found a kind of sugar cane.

Probably the sugar-cane plant that we know about today came from those long-ago reeds that grew in far-off India. Much of the sugar used today is made from the juice of the sugar cane.

There are many different plant families in the world, and sugar cane is a plant of the grass family. All kinds of grasses, large and small, belong to this family, but the sugar-cane plant is one of the giants of the family.

It grows to a height of seven to fifteen feet, and it has a long stem made up of many little sections or joints. Near the top of the stem there is a bunch of narrow, grasslike leaves.

As the thick-stemmed grass grows, the juice in its stalk becomes sweet and then sweeter. When at last the cane is ripe, after about seven to twenty-two months, this juice is crushed out and made into sugar.

Sugar cane grows only in very warm countries and needs plenty of water and a rich soil. It is the sun and the rain and the fertile soil that create the sweetness in the juice.

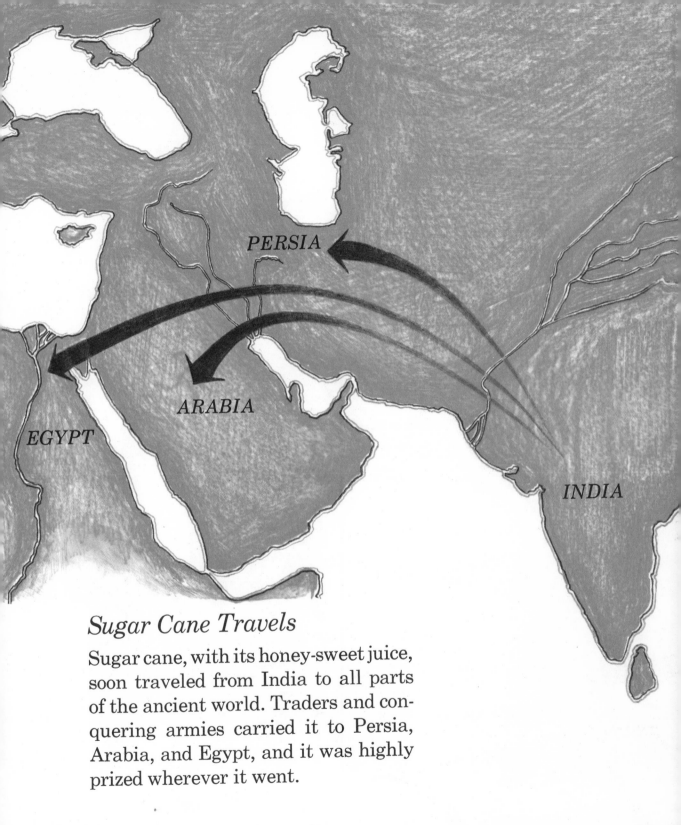

PERSIA

EGYPT

ARABIA

INDIA

Sugar Cane Travels

Sugar cane, with its honey-sweet juice, soon traveled from India to all parts of the ancient world. Traders and conquering armies carried it to Persia, Arabia, and Egypt, and it was highly prized wherever it went.

14

Once, when some Indian princes owed tribute money to an emperor of China, the Chinese emperor demanded that the tribute be paid in sugar instead of in gold! In those days sugar was rarer than any gold! Later, men were sent from China to India to find out how to produce sugar from sugar cane.

Still later, Marco Polo, who traveled from Italy to China, wrote of the sugar mills as one of the wonders of China.

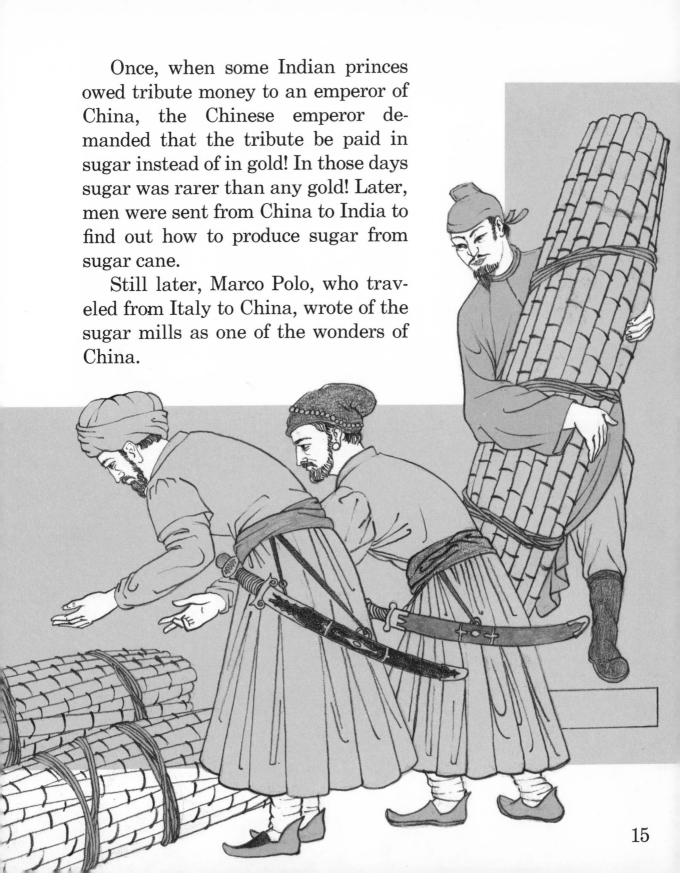

15

When the Crusaders returned from their attempts to capture the Holy City of Jerusalem, they brought back to their homes in Europe the knowledge of many things about which they had learned in the East. Among these was the strange new sweet called sugar. Soon a trade in sugar grew up between Europe and the East.

The sugar, wrapped in palm leaves and sewn up in cloth, traveled long, long distances on the backs of camels and in merchant ships with bright-colored sails to countries where it could not be grown because of the climate. But it cost so much that it was very precious, and only the princes and rich people were able to buy it.

The Early Sugar Traders

Venice was at one time, hundreds of years ago, the center of the sugar trade. Back and forth across the Mediterranean the merchant ships of Venice sailed, carrying precious cargoes of sugar and spices.

Pirates were always ready to attack these ships. Many battles were

18

fought, and many ships were lost. But sugar brought a great price, and so the Venetian traders grew rich.

A man living in Venice invented a way of making sugar into the form of a loaf. This was a great help to the sugar traders, and the inventor received many thousands of dollars for his discovery.

Sugar Cane in the New World

The people of Spain and Portugal saw that the Venetians were growing rich from their sugar trade with India.

They, too, wanted a share in the riches, and so they decided to find a new and shorter route to the land of sugar and spice. They wished to trade with India also.

Spanish and Portuguese sailors set out in their little, top-heavy sailing boats upon the unknown seas in search of a new route to India.

What they really found was a new world, whose fertile islands lay fair and green in the sea. Christopher Columbus, one of these sailors, named the islands, "The Indies," after India.

Columbus brought cuttings of sugar cane to the Indies when he made his second voyage there, about 1493, and he planted these in Santo Domingo. Also, the first sugar mill in what is now North America was built in 1508 near Santo Domingo.

The Spaniards who settled in these newly discovered islands found that the soil and the climate were just right for the sugar-cane plant. They set out

great sugar plantations in the Indies, which they cultivated with the help of their slaves.

Several years later, about 1530, the great Spanish conqueror, Cortes, carried the sugar cane to Mexico, and there he built sugar mills for making sugar in the new land.

Sugar cane also came to the part of the new world that is now the United States. The present city of New Orleans was at that time only a tiny settlement on the Gulf of Mexico.

One day the Brothers of a Jesuit monastery in New Orleans received a package from a monastery in Mexico. It contained a few plants of sugar cane. They set these out in their convent garden and watched over them, but the plants did not live in their new home.

Again, plants were sent to the Brothers in New Orleans from Mexico. This time a boy who knew how to care for sugar cane was sent with them. Under his care, the little plants grew and flourished.

This was the beginning of the great sugar plantations of the state of Louisiana.

Sugar Factory in Sicily — From a Print made in 1570

Old-Time Sugar Makers

Long ago men learned how to change the sweet juice of the sugar cane into sugar.

Old-time sugar makers crushed the juice from the cane stalks between heavy rollers.

They then poured the sweet, watery juice into open kettles and boiled it. As it boiled, it grew thicker and thicker, just as sugar and water do when these are boiled together to make candy. At last, it turned into a thick, sticky mass of sugar crystals and syrup.

This mass was packed into boxes or bags with holes in the bottom so that any of the syrupy water that remained might be drained out of it.

Soon only the sticky sugar crystals were left. These were molded into cone-shaped loaves of sugar and set up to dry.

This woodcut, made some four hundred years ago, pictures the whole process of old-time sugar making—from the donkey bringing in cane from the field to the sugar loaves stacked on the table.

The sugar that is brought in stores today is not in the form of loaf sugar, but is carefully packaged in boxes and bags.

In the Sugar-Cane Field

First, the cane is planted and tended in fields under a warm, southern sky. It grows tall and ripe, and the juice from which the sugar is made sweetens in the stalks until it is ready for the harvest.

At harvest time, workers go up and down the long rows of cane, cutting off the stalks by hand near where the stalks grow from the ground. Then, with another slash of a sharp, hooked knife they strip off the leaves.

The cut stalks are thrown into heaps and then loaded on carts or trucks which take them to the sugar mill if it is nearby. In some sugar-cane fields the stalks are carried on cars on a narrow-gauge railroad that runs from the field to the mill.

No time can be lost in harvesting, for the more quickly the cane is crushed after it is cut, the greater the amount of sweet juice that can be pressed from it.

In the Philippines, the gentle water buffalo, or *carabao,* is used to work in the sugar-cane field. The Philippines rank high among the world's sugar growers.

In Hawaii, the soil is so fertile that the sugar plantations yield the richest crop of sugar cane in the world. Hawaii does not refine or package its own sugar but ships it to the mainland of the United States in the form of raw sugar.

Harvester Loading
Sugar Cane

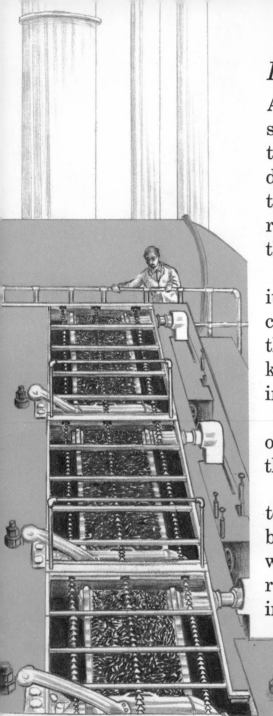

Raw Sugar

A sugar mill is usually built close to a sugar-cane field, and it is in this mill that raw sugar is made. All day long, during the busy harvest time, trucks, tractors, or the little narrow-gauge railroad cars come from the fields to the mill with loads of cane stalks.

When the cane arrives at the mill, it is dumped into a "washing" machine that cleans the stalks. From there it goes into a machine with sharp knives that "shred," or cut them into little pieces.

The stalks then go through a series of rollers that squeeze the cane so hard that the sweet juice flows out

Water is sprayed over the stalks to dissolve any more juice that might be in them. Next, that mixture of water and juice is heated; then it is run into tanks where any impurities in it are taken out.

A series of rollers squeeze the juice from the shredded cane.

The juice is next put into vacuum pans that reduce the juice until it becomes a mixture of crystals of sugar mixed with dark, sticky syrup. This syrup is known as molasses and must be removed from the sugar crystals.

This may seem like a hard task, but it is a simple job for the machinery of a sugar mill. The mixture of sugar crystals and molasses is put into huge machines where it is whirled about at a great rate of speed. The spinning motion separates the crystals of sugar from the molasses. The brownish crystals that are left are called raw sugar.

Filters (made of layers of cloth) inside a metal case strain out impurities from juice of the sugar cane.

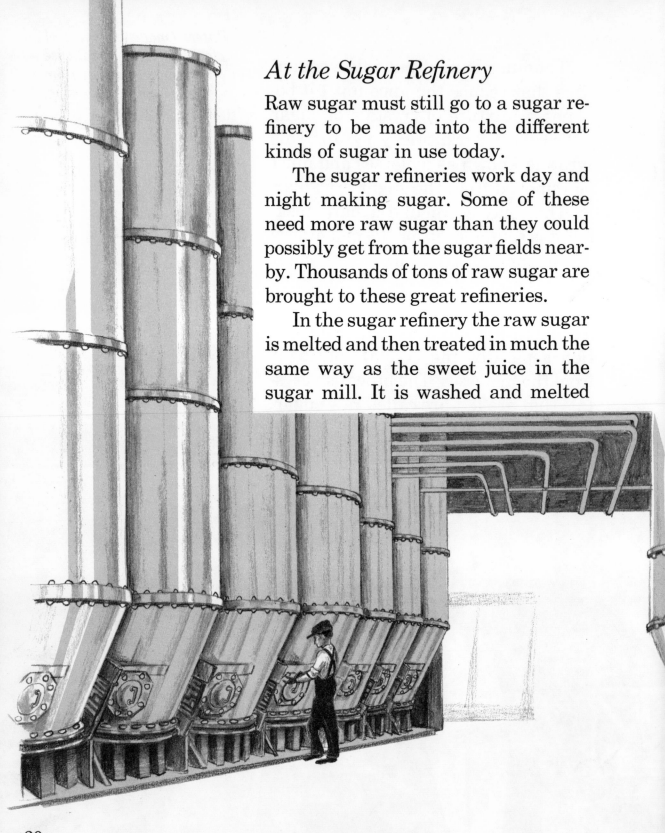

At the Sugar Refinery

Raw sugar must still go to a sugar refinery to be made into the different kinds of sugar in use today.

The sugar refineries work day and night making sugar. Some of these need more raw sugar than they could possibly get from the sugar fields nearby. Thousands of tons of raw sugar are brought to these great refineries.

In the sugar refinery the raw sugar is melted and then treated in much the same way as the sweet juice in the sugar mill. It is washed and melted and again purified in great tanks and pans. It is then strained and boiled.

This time the sugar crystals that have been formed are white and glistening. These crystals are pure sugar. They are then dried and sifted through screens into different-sized crystals and sold as granulated sugar.

Some of the sugar, before it dries completely, is pressed and then cut into cubes and tablets. Some when dry, is ground into finest powder known as confectioners' sugar, and is used in making icings and candies.

Products from Sugar

There has been little waste in making sugar from cane. Much of the fiber of the stalks that remains after the juice is crushed out is used as fuel to keep the giant machines running.

That fiber is also made into a kind of wallboard used to make or cover walls and ceilings instead of wooden boards or plaster.

The white powdery material that covers a sugar-cane stalk is used to make the carbon paper used in business offices.

Chemists also make a material from sugar that will toughen plastics and keep them from breaking.

Sugar, in one form or another, is also used in many drugs and dyes.

Monosodium glutamate, a white crystal-like powder, often used in cooking to bring out the flavor of food, is made from the molasses from sugar beets.

The by-products of sugar are numerous. Even some types of nylon fiber are made from a substance that is obtained by treating sugar-cane fibers with acid.

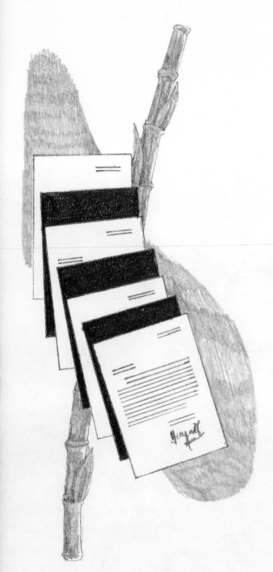

The Discovery of Beet Sugar

Sugar made from sugar cane is not the only type of sugar we have today.

In 1879 a German chemist, and later an American chemist discovered that sugar could be made from the juice of beets. The "whitish" beets with sugar in the juice in their roots are called "sugar beets." These beets belong to the same family as the red beets that grow in our gardens and are used as a vegetable.

Sugar cane needs a hot sun, but sugar beets can grow in a cool climate. This means that people in these countries can raise beets and make their own sugar, and not have to bring it from other lands.

France was one nation that always had to obtain the sugar she used from other countries. At the time of Napoleon a war was being waged between France and Great Britain. When ships tried to go into French ports with their cargoes of sugar, they found that the British ships had blockaded the harbors and would not let them enter. France would just have to go without sugar!

The French people had heard the story of the chemists' ability to obtain

sugar from beets. So in 1811, Napoleon, the French emperor, granted land and money to his people so that they could raise sugar beets and build sugar mills and refineries. In this way France could produce the sugar she needed.

It was hard for the French people to believe that sugar could be made from beets. A picture of Napoleon shows him squeezing the juice of a sugar beet into his coffee. The baby prince is chewing a beet. The nurse, who does not believe that sugar could come from a beet, says, "Suck, my dear! Your father calls it sugar."

Machinery being loaded onto river boats at New Orleans.

Today the greatest number of sugar beets are grown in the cold, dry sections of the north central part of the United States and Europe.

Russia grows the greatest number of sugar beets, producing over eighty-eight million tons in each year. United States is second, France is third, and West Germany is fourth.

Beet Sugar in the United States

The people in the United States who first tried to grow beets and make sugar had a hard time. They knew little about growing the beets or about the machinery needed to make the sugar.

The machinery for one of the first beet-sugar mills was brought from France. It traveled across the ocean and landed at the port of New Orleans where the Mississippi River flows into the Gulf of Mexico. There it was loaded on river boats and carried up the river for many days. There were no railroads and few roads at that time. So it was pulled over wild, rough country in oxcarts to the western land where the sugar mill was to be built. This sugar mill failed, for the sugar that was first made from the sugar beet was so bitter that it could not be eaten.

Again and again American farmers tried to raise the beets and produce sugar. At last they did succeed. The sugar beets grew and flourished. The sugar mills turned out beet sugar as fine and white and sweet as any sugar.

One-third of the sugar consumed in the United States is beet sugar.

Harvester Loading Beets

Sugar from Sugar Beets

Before beet seed can be planted, the soil must be prepared very carefully. A beet plant will not grow well unless it finds exactly the kind of nourishment it needs in the earth. When this nourishment is gone, the next crop of beets must be grown in a new field.

The seeds are sown in the spring. The sun warms them, and the rain waters them. When the little green shoots appear above the ground, the farmer and his helpers thin these out and cultivate them with the greatest care.

In about a year the beets are grown, and the tops are large and green. The juice in the beet root becomes ripe and sweet. It is time for the harvest.

Men and machines dig the beets from the ground and cut the green tops from the whitish roots. The beet roots are loaded into wagons and trucks and trains and taken to the sugar-beet factory, where beet sugar is made.

In the factory great scrubbing machines wash them clean. Knives, turned by machinery, cut the beets into thin slices. The slices are then soaked in great tanks of hot water until all the sweet juice is taken from them.

In the refinery, this sugar-beet juice is made into sugar that is fine and white and glistening, and sweet to the taste.

The fresh green tops cut from the beets are not left to waste in the field. The cows and the sheep and the lambs grow strong and fat on this food.

The beet pulp from the sugar factory and the molasses, or syrup, are also prepared into food for the farm animals.

Even the soil in which the sugar beet has been grown is used to grow many other plants.

Digging and cutting beets at the turn of the century.

39

Boiling Sap, From an Old
Engraving

Sugar from a Tree

Besides sugar from the sugar cane and the sugar beet, there is a small supply of another kind of sugar. This is maple sugar made from the sap of the sugar-maple tree.

When the white men first settled North America, they found the Indians making and using maple sugar. Soon they learned how to do this, too.

In order to obtain the maple syrup, holes are drilled in the trunks of the sugar-maple tree in the very early spring. Little funnels or short pipes are fitted into the holes. The watery sap that runs out through the funnels is caught in buckets hung on the trees.

This sweet sap is boiled down in open kettles until it becomes rich maple syrup. When it is boiled for a longer time, it becomes maple sugar.

The sugar-maple tree lives a long time, but its growth is very slow. It takes about forty years before a tree is ready to be tapped, so the amount of maple sugar that can be made is very small compared with the amount of other sugar manufactured.

It takes about thirty-five gallons of sap from a sugar-maple tree to make one gallon of syrup. And a tree yields, at best, about forty gallons of sap in one season.

In Place of Sugar

There are many substitutes for sugar that are sold in tremendous quantities today. None of these sugar substitutes has any food value. They do nothing

to supply energy and heat to our bodies, as does real sugar. However, many of these manufactured substitutes are helpful to a person when it would be harmful for him to use sugar. Also many people, particularly women, use sugar substitutes in their tea or coffee, or other foods, in order to keep down their weight.

One of the best known sugar substitutes is saccharin. This is a white crystal powder made from a mixture of coal tar and petroleum. It is much sweeter than sugar, but it definitely has no value as a food. It is also sometimes used in cooking.

Saccharin is available in drugstores, most grocery stores and supermarkets in tablets or in liquid form. It is only one of the many trademarked artificial sweeteners now manufactured, all of which contain some saccharin.

Extensive studies are now being made to determine whether the overuse of such products may be harmful to a person's health.

Sugar as a Food

When man learned how to extract the juice from the sugar cane and from the

sugar beet, he produced a food that not only tastes good but is also valuable for the growth of our bodies.

Sugar is one of man's most important foods. Just as gasoline provides power for an automobile, sugar supplies heat and energy for our bodies.

As a food, a person can use as much as ninety-five pounds a year! Of course, not all that amount is sprinkled on cereal nor used to sweeten tea and coffee. Much of it is used in soft drinks, baked goods, such as pies and cakes, in desserts, in canned fruits, in candy, ice cream, and jams and jellies.

When sugar was first produced, it was very rare and very costly. Now, sugar is something that almost everyone can have and enjoy.

Index